PERSONALITY PROFILES

KIMBERLY

What's in a Name?

MATTHEW ♥ AMANDA

What Your Name Says About You!

MADISON ♥ TAYL

Written By Vivian Fernandez
Design & Illustration By Amy McIntyre

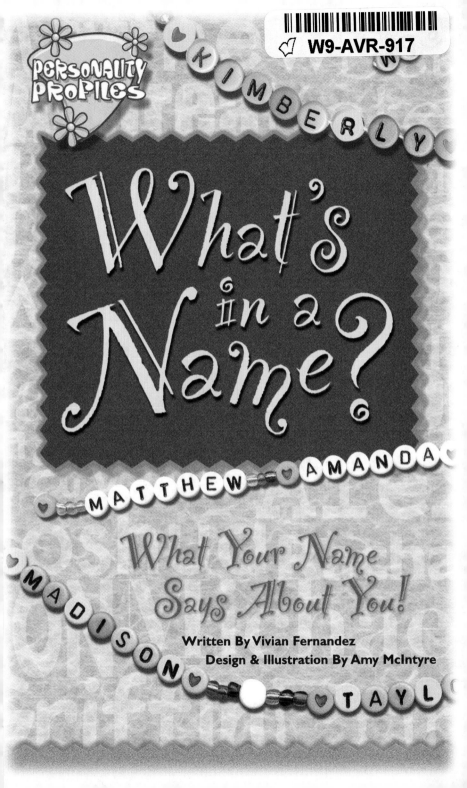

ISBN 1-931623-10-4

Written by Vivian Fernandez

Cover Design by Amy McIntyre
Design by Amy McIntyre

Contents

Chapter 1

How Did You Get Your Name?

How many times a day do you hear your name? If you're an average kid, it's probably a lot. Whether you're being called to eat dinner, or being reminded that you're going to be late for school if you don't hurry up, or being asked if you finished your homework, your name is probably the one word you hear the most.

Your name is an important part of who you are. It's how the world knows you. Sometimes, it's the very first thing someone knows about you.

But how did you get your name? Is it an old family name? Did your parents have a good friend they wanted to name you after? Did your parents look in a baby-name book and find a name with a meaning they liked? Or maybe your parents followed a baby-naming tradition.

No matter how your parents chose your name, your name has a meaning and a past. Some names are thousands of years old, some are brand-new—created just for you. Your name may even have first been used in a country you've never been to, by people who speak a different language than you!

In this book, you'll learn lots of things about names—interesting traditions for naming babies, the most popular names around the world, what names mean, and what last names say about a family's history. You'll even be able to play some name games to come up with a pirate name, a secret agent name, and more.

Did you know that some countries have a list of names parents must choose from when they name their babies? Or that some people don't like to use the names of living relatives when naming a baby? Read about the different reasons some parents have for choosing a name for their children.

Sometimes, creative parents come up with original names for their children. These names start out as one-of-a-kind, but quickly become popular because they sound beautiful. Created names are very much in style with African American families. Many times, the new names are based on a traditional name, but with a new beginning or ending. To make the names unique, parents might add Chan-, Shan-, Ka-, La-, De-, or Da to the beginning. Or they might add -isha, -on, -won, or -quon to the end of the name.

Some Popular African American Names

GIRLS	BOYS
Aeisha	Dajuan
Chandelle	Datwon
Jaleesa	DeMarcus
Jonava	Deonte
Kaneesha	Jawan
Keisha	Keshon
Kishanda	Lamonte
LaQuanda	LeQuann
Shaneika	Quantray
Shavonda	Rondre
Shayleen	Shawnel
Tanisha	Tequan

Imagine having three cousins all with the same first name as you. It could happen if you lived in Greece. That's because it's tradition for parents to name their kids after grandparents. The first son is named after his father's father, and the second son is named after his mother's father. And it's the same pattern for girls—the first daughter is named after her father's mother, the second daughter is named after her mother's mother. Any other children are named after other favorite relatives.

Because cousins in the same family share grandparents, there might be five Sophia's at family get-togethers. This would make things very confusing if someone yelled out, "Sophia! Come here!" To make things a little less confusing, Greek parents might give children their own names as middle names. So, Damalis, the daughter of Philippos and Lucia, would be Damalis Lucia. Her cousin, the daughter of Damalis's sister Helene, would be Damalis Helene.

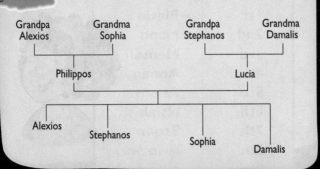

Family Tree

| Grandpa Alexios | Grandma Sophia | | Grandpa Stephanos | Grandma Damalis |

Philippos — Lucia

Alexios   Stephanos   Sophia   Damalis

In the African country of Ghana, you might know what day of the week someone was born on and how many brothers or sisters he has just by hearing his name. In the Ghanaian tradition, a baby is named after the day of the week he was born. He might also get a second name that tells what order in the family he was born. If you look at the charts below, you can see that the second son born on a Wednesday would have the name Kweku Manu. (*There are many tribes in Ghana, and different tribes have different names for the week and birth order. This is just one example.*)

WEEKDAY	BOY	GIRL
Sunday	Kwesi	Esi
Monday	Kojo	Adjon
Tuesday	Kobina	Abena
Wednesday	Kweku	Ekua
Thursday	Yaw	Yaa
Friday	Kofi	Efua
Saturday	Kwame	Ama

BIRTH ORDER	NAME
1st	Piesie
2nd	Manu
3rd	Mensah
4th	Annan
5th	Anum
6th	Nsiah
7th	Esuon
8th	Awotwe
9th	Nkrumah
10th	Badn

Not so long ago, most Japanese girls were given names with -ko, which means "a child," at the end of their names. But now more and more parents are choosing names that are less traditional. Now, Momoko, Riko, Sakurako, and Nanako are the only names ending in -ko that are in the list of 100 popular names for Japanese girls.

If your parents followed Chinese tradition, you and your brothers and sisters would all have names that started with the same sound. So if your name is Kazuko, your brother's name might be Kadon. In this way, the Chinese show their family ties.

Believe it or not, France has a law about which names parents can give their babies. The law was made in 1803, and it said that all French babies had to have French names with French spellings. Through the years, names have been added to the list. Now the list includes some names from other countries, names from nature, and more.

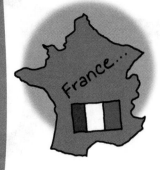

France...

In some cultures, such as Chinese and Hawaiian, people believe that evil spirits might steal a baby. To keep the spirits away, a parent gives their baby a fake name in addition to the "real" name. These fake names have ugly meanings, or are names that don't sound good. Parents hope that the spirits will think the baby is as disgusting as the name, and will leave the baby alone.

Many Native American tribes follow the tradition of giving names at important times in someone's life. An adult might have a name completely different from the name he was given when he was born, or the name he had when he was a child. Native American names are often based on nature (such as Hula, which means "eagle") or on something the person did (such as Wyandanch, which means "the wise speaker").

HAWAII....

Many Jewish families name their children after relatives. But they don't like to use the names of relatives that are still alive— they believe that's bad luck.

Chapter 2

Top 10 Names Around the World

W ant to know if your name is popular in Australia? The following lists show the 10 most popular names for babies born in 2002 in several different countries. Did your name make the list?

AUSTRALIA	
Girls	Boys
1 Emily	Joshua
2 Jessica	Lachlan
3 Chloe	Jack
4 Isabella	Thomas
5 Sarah	Ethan
6 Sophie	James
7 Olivia	Daniel
8 Georgia	Nicholas
9 Grace	William
10 Hannah	Benjamin

CANADA

Girls	Boys
1 Emily	Ethan
2 Emma	Joshua
3 Hannah	Matthew
4 Sarah	Jacob
5 Jessica	Nicholas
6 Madison	Justin
7 Olivia	Ryan
8 Grace	Benjamin
9 Megan	Liam
10 Isabella	Alexander

ENGLAND

Girls	Boys
1 Chloe	Jack
2 Emily	Jashua
3 Jessica	Thomas
4 Ellie	James
5 Sophie	Daniel
6 Megan	Benjamin
7 Charlotte	William
8 Lucy	Samuel
9 Hannah	Joseph
10 Olivia	Oliver

GERMANY

Girls	Boys
1 Marie	Alexander
2 Sophie	Maximilian
3 Maria	Paul
4 Anna	Leon
5 Laura	Lukas
6 Lea	Jonas
7 Katherina	Tim
8 Sarah	David
9 Julia	Niklas
10 Lena	Luca

SCOTLAND

Girls	Boys
1 Chloe	Jack
2 Sophie	Lewis
3 Emma	Cameron
4 Amy	Ryan
5 Erin	James
6 Ellie	Jamie
7 Rachel	Liam
8 Lauren	Mathew
9 Megan	Ross
10 Hannah	Callum

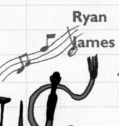

SWITZERLAND

Girls	Boys
1 Julia	Filip
2 Emma	Oscar
3 Wilma	William
4 Hanna	Viktor
5 Elin	Simon
6 Linnea	Anton
7 Amanda	Erik
8 Ida	Alexander
9 Matilda	Emil
10 Moa	Lucas

UNITED STATES

Girls	Boys
1 Emily	Jacob
2 Madison	Michael
3 Emma	Joshua
4 Hannah	Matthew
5 Alexis	Ethan
6 Ashley	Joseph
7 Abigail	Andrew
8 Sarah	Christopher
9 Samantha	Daniel
10 Olivia	Nicholas

Chapter 3

What's in a Name?

In this chapter, you can look up your name and find out where it was first used, what your name means, and some variations of your name. The names are separated into two sections. The section with girl names begins on page 16. The section with boy names begins on page 50. Names are listed alphabetically.

How to read each entry:

Andrea (Greek) strong *Also*: **Andree, Andria**

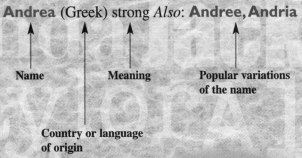

Name   Meaning   Popular variations of the name

Country or language of origin

★ Famous...

Abigail (Hebrew) a father's joy *Also*: **Abagail, Abby, Avigail**

Aeisha (Arabic) life *Also*: **Aisha, Asiah, Ayeesha**

Aiko (Japanese) little one

Alana (Irish) peaceful; beautiful *Also*: **Alaina, Alannah, Alayna**

beautiful...

Aleeka (African) pretty girl

Alexandra (Greek) defender of people *Also*: **Alejandra, Aleka, Alexa, Alexi, Alexis**

Alice (Old German) noble *Also*: **Alison, Allie, Allyce**

Alicia (Greek) truthful *Also*: **Alisha, Allison, Ilysha**

Aliyah (Hebrew) to go up *Also*: **Aaliyah, Alya**

Alva (Spanish) white; pure *Also*: **Alvah, Alvy, Elva**

Ⓐ Ⓛ Ⓥ Ⓐ

This is the middle name of a famous male inventor — **Thomas Alva Edison.**

Alyssa (Greek) sensible

Amanda (Latin) much loved *Also*: **Amata, Mandi, Mandy**

Amber (English) a yellowish, semi-transparent stone

Amelie (Old German) hard working *Also*: **Amelia, Amelinda, Amella**

Amy (Latin) much loved *Also*: **Aimee, Aimie, Amada, Amata, Amil**

LOVED

Anastasia (Greek) resurrection
Also: **Anastacia, Anastase, Anastazia**

Andrea (Greek) strong
Also: **Andree, Andria**

Angela (Greek) messenger
of God *Also*: **Angelica, Angelina, Angelique, Angie**

Ann (Hebrew) graceful *Also*: **Ana, Anissa, Anita, Anna, Anne, Annette, Annie**

Antoinette (Latin) priceless *Also*: **Antonia, Toni**

Ariel (Hebrew) lion of God *Also*: **Aeriel, Ari, Arielle**

Ashley (Old English) ash tree meadow
Also: **Ashlee, Ashleigh, Ashly, Ashlyn, Ashton**

Audrey (Old English) noble; strong *Also*: **Audie, Audra, Audre, Audreen**

(A)(M)(Y)

Other "Much Loved" Names

Cher (French)

Daryl (English)

Esme (French)

Suki (Japanese)

Trudy (German)

graceful!

Azura (French) blue sky
Also: **Azure**

Bailey (English) person in charge *Also*: **Babb, Babbette, Babe, Barb, Barbie, Basha, Varenka, Vava**

Beatrice (Latin) she makes others happy *Also*: **Bea, Beatrix, Beatriz, Bebe**

Belinda (English) combination name from Belle (beautiful) and Linda (pretty) *Also*: **Belynda**

Belle (French) beautiful *Also*: **Bella**

Bernice (Greek) she brings victory *Also*: **Bema, Berenice, Bernelle, Bernetta, Bernette, Bernicia, Bernyce**

Bethany (Arabic) house of the poor *Also*: **Bethanie, BethAnn, Bethanny**

Beverly (English) beaver stream *Also*: **Bev, Beverelle, Beverley**

Bianca (Italian) white *Also*: **Biancha, Blanca, Blanche**

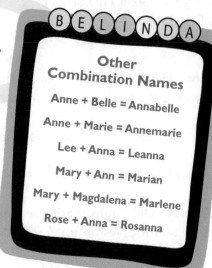

B E L I N D A

Other Combination Names

Anne + Belle = Annabelle

Anne + Marie = Annemarie

Lee + Anna = Leanna

Mary + Ann = Marian

Mary + Magdalena = Marlene

Rose + Anna = Rosanna

strong

Blair (Scottish) someone who lives on low, flat ground *Also*: **Blaire, Blayr, Blayre**

Bonnie (English) good *Also*: **Boni, Bonne, Bonnebell, Bonnie, Bonny**

Bradley (Old English) a wide meadow *Also*: **Brad, Bradleigh, Bradly**

Breanna (Irish) strong *Also*: **Breann, Bree, Brianna, Bryanna**

Brenda (English) sword; on fire *Also*: **Bren, Brenndah**

Other "Strong" Names

Abira (Hebrew)

Andra (Scottish)

Brites (Portuguese)

Etana (Hebrew)

Valentina (Latin)

Brett (English) someone from Britain

Bridget (Irish) strong *Also*: **Birgit, Bridgette, Brigida, Brigitte, Brygida**

Brittany (Latin) someone from England *Also*: **Britany, Britney**

Brooke (English) small stream *Also*: **Brook**

Caitlin (Irish) pure *Also*: **Caitlyn, Kaitlyn, Katelynn**

Camille (Latin) helper in the church *Also*: **Cami, Camilla, Cammylle**

Candace (Latin) white; glowing *Also*: **Candee, Candice, Kandys**

Caroline (Latin) woman *Also*: **Carla, Carly, Carol, Carolina, Carlota, Carolyn, Carrie, Karolyn**

Casey (Irish) observant *Also*: **Cassie, Cacey, Kacia**

Cassandra (Greek) helper of people; protector *Also*: **Cass, Cassandre, Kasandra**

Cassidy (Irish) clever

Catherine (English) pure *Also*: **Catalina, Catarina, Cathie, Caty**

Cecilia (Latin) blind *Also*: **Cecily, Celia, Celine, Sheila, Sissy**

Celeste (Latin) heavenly *Also*: **Cela**

Charleze (French) womanly *Also*: **Charlize**

blooming...

C H L O E

Chloe is a very popular name in England. It was the number one choice for girls born in the years 1998, 1999, 2000, 2001, and 2002!

Charlotte (French) a small woman *Also*: **Caitlan, Catlin, Kaitlyn, Katelynn**

bright...

Chelsea (English) a ship's port *Also*: **Chelsa, Chelsy**

Chloe (Greek) blooming

Christine (English) anointed one *Also*: **Chris, Christina, Christy, Tina**

Clara (Greek) bright *Also*: **Clair, Clarice, Clarissa, Klara, Klaryssa**

Claudia (Latin) limping; weak *Also*: **Claudette, Claudine**

Colette (Greek) victorious people *Also*: **Coletta**

Colleen (Gaelic) girl *Also*: **Colene**

Courtney (English) someone from the king's court *Also*: **Cortney, Courtnie**

Crystal (Greek) ice; gem *Also*: **Christal, Krystle**

Cynthia (Greek) moon *Also*: **Cindi, Cindy**

Daisy (English) flower name that means "eye of the day" *Also*: **Dacey, Daisha**

Dakota (Native American) friend

Dalila (African) gentle *Also*: **Dalia**

Dana (English) someone from Denmark *Also*: **Daina, Danee, Denae**

Danielle (Hebrew) God is my judge *Also*: **Danee, Danela, Dania, Daniella, Danika**

Daphne (Greek) laurel tree

Dara (Hebrew) wisdom *Also*: **Darice, Darrah**

Darlene (English) darling *Also*: **Dacey, Daisha**

Dawn (English) sunrise *Also*: **Dawna, Dawnetta**

D A I S Y

Other Flower Names:

Amaryllis (Greek)
Camellia (English)
Chrysanthemum (Greek)
Dahlia (Scandinavian)
Faghira (Arabic)
Iantha (Greek)
Jacinth (Greek)
Linnea (Scandinavian)

Deborah (Hebrew) bee *Also*: **Deb, Debby, Debra**

Deirdre (Irish) fear; anger; sadness *Also*: **Dedra, Deidra, Deirdra, Diedre**

Denise (Greek) from Dionysius, the god of wine in Greek mythology *Also*: **Denese, Deni, Denice, Denys**

Destiny (French) fate

Diana (Latin) sacred; like God *Also*: **Dee, Diane, Didi**

Dolores (Spanish) sadness
Also: **Delores**

Donna (Italian) lady
Also: **Dahna, Donielle, Donetta, Donya**

Dorothy (Greek) gift from God
Also: **Dora, Dorthea, Dot, Dotty**

Eileen (Irish) bright *Also*: **Aileen, Ilene**

Elaine (French) shining *Also*: **Alayna, Elana, Eleana**

Eleanor (Greek) light
Also: **Eleonora, Ellinor**

Elizabeth (Hebrew) promised to God *Also*: **Babette, Bess, Beth, Betsey, Elisa, Elisabeta, Eliza, Elsbeth, Lisa, Ysabel**

Ella (German) all; completely

D E N I S E

Other Names from Mythology:

Athena goddess of wisdom

Aurora goddess of the dawn

Chloris goddess of flowers

Hermione from Hermes, messenger of the gods

Luna goddess of the moon

Nike goddess of victory

E I L E E N

Before she changed her name, Eileen Regina Edwards was the name of singer

a. Faith Hill

b. Reba McEntire

c. Shania Twain

c. Shania Twain

Ellen (English) light
Also: **Elan, Elyn**

Elizabeth was one of the 10 most popular names in the United States for the years 1990-2001.

ELIZABETH

Elsa (Spanish) noble *Also*: **Emilie**

Emily (German) hardworking

Emma (German) accepting everything

Erica (Scandinavian) ruler for all time *Also*: **Erika**

Erin (Gaelic) from Ireland *Also*: **Erene, Eryn**

Estelle (Latin) star *Also*: **Estee, Esther, Estrella, Stella**

Evelyn (Irish) life *Also*: **Evelyne**

Faiza (Arabic) winner

Fatima (Arabic) daughter of the prophet Muhammad

Felicia (Latin) happy; lucky *Also*: **Felice, Felicity**

FELICIA

Other "Happy" Names
Ada (English)
Bliss (English)
Duscha (Russian)
Fareeha (Arabic)

Fiona (Irish) pale

Frances (Latin) someone from France *Also*: **Fanny, Fran, Francesca, Francie, Frannie**

Frederique (German) peace; king *Also*: **Freddie, Frederica**

Gabrielle (Hebrew) God is my strength *Also*: **Gabby, Gabriela**

Gail (Hebrew) my father rejoices *Also*: **Gayle**

Galiena (German) high one

Genevieve (Celtic) white; woman

Geraldine (French) one who rules with a spear *Also*: **Geralyn, Geri**

Gertrude (German) with the strength of a spear *Also*: **Gertie, Trudey**

Gila (Hebrew) joy

Gilda (English) covered thinly with gold

Gina (Hebrew) garden *Also*: **Geena**

Giselle (German) promise *Also*: **Gisela**

Other "Golden" Names
Aurelia (Latin)
Dior (French)
Eldora (Spanish)
Golda (English)
Hemali (Hindu)
Nudar (Arabic)
Ora (Spanish)
Paza (Hebrew)

Gladys (Welsh) with a limp; weak

Gloria (Latin) glory
Also: **Gabby, Gabriela**

Grace (Latin) grace
Also: **Gracia, Graziella**

Gretchen (German) pearl

Gwyneth (Welsh) happiness; blessed *Also*: **Gwenyth, Gwynn**

Hadiya (Arabic) gift

Hadley (English) meadow

Haley (English) hay meadow
Also: **Hailey, Halli, Hayley**

Hallie (German) someone who rules

Halimah (Arabic) gentle

Hana (Japanese) flower

Hanh (Vietnamese) ethical

Hannah (Hebrew) grace *Also*: **Hana**

Harriet (German) leader of the house
Also: **Harrie, Harrietta, Hattie**

Haru (Japanese) born in spring *Also*: **Haruko**

Heidi (German) noble

Helen (Greek) light
Also: **Helena, Helene**

Helga (German) holy

Hilary (Greek) glad; cheerful

Hilda (German) woman of battle

Holly (English) plant

H O P E

The meanings of some names, such as Hope, are based on character traits, or virtues, people believe are important to have. Other virtue names include Amity, Bliss, Charity, Faith, Grace, Harmony, Joy, and Patience.

I M A N

Other "Faithful" Names

Amana (Hebrew)

Fae (English)

Fidelia (Spanish)

Leala (French)

Wafa (Arabic)

Hope (English) to wish for something to happen

Ida (English) successful

Ilana (Hebrew) oak tree

Iman (Arabic) faith; belief
Also: **Imani**

Imelda (German) fierce battle

Inez (Spanish) pure *Also*: **Ines, Ynez**

Ingrid (Scandinavian) beautiful

Ione (Greek) violet flower

Irene (Greek) peace *Also*:
Arina, Eirin, Orya, Rina, Yaryna

Iris (Greek) rainbow

Irma (German) complete

Isabel (Spanish) promise of God *Also*: **Isa, Isabeau, Isabella, Isabelle, Ysabel**

Ivana (Hebrew) God is gracious

Ivy (Greek) from the ivy plant *Also*: **Ivyanne**

Jacqueline (French) he who replaces *Also*: **Jackie, Jaclynn**

Jade (Spanish) green gemstone *Also*: **Jada, Jayde**

Jaimie (French) one who replaces *Also*: **Jaime, Jamie**

Jamila (Arabic) beautiful *Also*: **Jamille**

Jan (Hebrew) God is good
Also: **Jana, Janina, Janna**

Jane (English) God's grace
Also: **Janet, Janice, Janie, Jayne**

Jasmine (Persian) flower
Also: **Jasmeen, Jessamine, Yasmine**

Jean (Scottish) God is good *Also*: **Jeana, Jeanette, Jeannie**

Jena (Arabic) little bird

Jennifer (Welsh) white; soft *Also*: **Genn, Jen, Jena, Jenalyn, Jeny**

Jessica (Hebrew) he sees; God's grace *Also*: **Jess, Jesse**

Jill (English) young

Joanne is the first name of J.K. Rowling — creator of Harry Potter.

Joan (Hebrew) God is good *Also*: **Joanie, Joni**

Joanne (English) God is good *Also*: **Joana, Joanna**

Jocelyn (Latin) happy

Jodi (Hebrew) praised *Also*: **Jodie, Jody**

Jordan (Hebrew) to go down

Joyce (Latin) joyous

Julia (Latin) young *Also*: **Jula, Julie**

JULIETTE

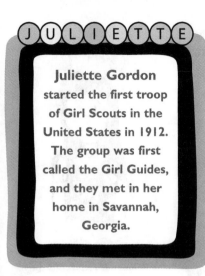

Juliette Gordon started the first troop of Girl Scouts in the United States in 1912. The group was first called the Girl Guides, and they met in her home in Savannah, Georgia.

Juliette (French) downy; soft-haired; youthful
Also: **Juliet, Julieta, Julita**

Justine (Latin) fair

Kai (Hawaiian) sea

Kaitlyn (Irish) pure
Also: **Kaitlyn, Katelin**

Kamilla (Arabic) perfect
Also: **Kameela, Kamla**

Kara (Latin) dear *Also*: **Kaira, Karalee, Kari**

Karen (Scandanavian) pure

Katherine (Greek) pure
Also: **Katalina, Kate, Katerina, Katharyn, Kathleen, Kathy, Katie, Katrina, Kit**

KATE

Kates Who Act
Kate Beckinsale
Kate Hudson
Kate Winslet
Katie Holmes

Kayla (English) pure
Also: **Kaela, Kaelee**

Kelly (Irish) warrior

Kelsey (English) island

Kendra (English) knowledge *Also*: **Kena**

Kerry (Irish) country in Ireland

Kimberly (English) king's meadow *Also*: **Kim, Kimba, Kimball, Kimber**

Kirsten (Scandinavian) anointed
Also: **Kerstie, Kiersten, Kirsta**

Kora (Greek) girl *Also*: **Cora, Coralyn, Corinne, Koreen, Korette, Kory**

Korina (English) maiden

Kristen (Greek) anointed
Also: **Krista, Kristina, Kristene**

Lacey (Latin) cheerful
Also: **Lacie**

Laine (English) bright one *Also*: **Lainey, Layne**

Lana (English) pretty
Also: **Lanae**

Lara (English) famous
Also: **Larinda**

L A U R A

Laura Ingalls Wilder was the writer of the "Little House" series of books. The books are based on her life growing up in the Midwest United States in the 1870s and 1880s. The first book in the series is *Little House in the Big Woods*.

Larissa (Greek) happy
Also: **Laryssa**

Laura (Latin) laurel
Also: **Laural, Lauren, Laurie, Lora, Loren, Lori**

Leah (Hebrew) tired *Also*: **Lea, Leia**

Leena (Hindu) devoted

Leigh (English) meadow
Also: **Lee**

Leila (Arabic) dark as
night *Also*: **Laila, Leela**

Lena (Greek) light *Also*: **Lina**

Lenore (Greek) like a lion
Also: **Leanore, Lenora**

Other
Animal Names
Bernadette (French) bear
Leandra (Latin) lion
Orlenda (Russian) eagle
Panya (African) mouse
Yael (Hebrew) goat

LENORE

Leslie (English) low meadow *Also*: **Lesly**

Glad...

Letitia (Latin) glad
Also: **Leticia**

Linda (Spanish) pretty
Also: **Lynda, Lynn**

Lindsey (English) island of
linden trees *Also*: **Lindsay**

Lisa (Hebrew) promised to God *Also*: **Leeza, Lisette, Liza**

Lola (Spanish) strong woman *Also*: **Lolita**

Lorraine (French) area in France

Louise (German) famous soldier
Also: **Aloise, Louisa, Luisa**

France...

Lourdes (French) area in France

Lucy (Latin) light *Also*: **Lucille, Lucinda**

Lovable...

Mabel (English) lovable
Also: **Mabelle, Maybel**

Mackenzie (Irish)
daughter of a wise leader

Madeline (Hebrew)
woman from Magdala in
Greece *Also*: **Maddie,
Madelaine, Madge,
Magda**

Madison (English) son of the mighty ruler

Magdalene (Spanish) woman from Magdala, an area in the
Middle East

Mai (Japanese) everyone

Maia (Greek) mother

Mallory (French) unlucky *Also*: **Malori**

Marcia (Latin) warlike *Also*: **Marce,
Marcela, Marcie, Marsha**

Margaret (Greek) pearl
Also: **Greta, Gretal, Maggie,
Margarita, Margery,
Marguerite, Meg, Megan,
Meghan, Rita**

Sorrowful...

Mariah (Hebrew) sorrowful

Marie (French) bitterness

Marissa (Latin) the sea

Martha (Arabic) lady *Also*: **Macia, Marta, Mattie**

Mary (Hebrew) bitter *Also*: **Maria, Marial, Moira, Molly**

One of the best-known horror stories was written by a woman named **Mary Shelley.** Her friends challenged her to write a ghost story and she came up with a great one — Frankenstein. She was only nineteen years old when she completed the story.

Matilda (German) mighty warrior *Also*: **Maddie, Mathilde, Matty, Maude, Tilda, Tilly**

Maureen (Irish) bitterness *Also*: **Moreen**

Melanie (Greek) dark-skinned *Also*: **Mel, Melany**

Melissa (Greek) bee

Bee...

Mercedes (Spanish) mercy

Michelle (French) who is like God

Mirabel (Latin) wonderful; very beautiful *Also*: **Mirabella**

Miranda (Latin) admirable; strange; wonderful; miracle *Also*: **Randi**

Miriam (Hebrew) bitter

Monica (Latin) adviser *Also*: **Monique**

Very Beautiful...

NANCY

Nancys in Sports

Nancy Drolet
Hockey

Nancy Greene
Skiing

Nancy Kerrigan
Figure skating

Nancy Lieberman
Basketball

Nancy Lopez
Golf

Montana (Spanish) mountain; also, a state in the United States

Montana

Morgan (Welsh) bright; edge of the sea *Also*: **Morgana**

Muriel (Irish) bright as the sea *Also*: **Murielle**

Nadia (Russian) hope *Also*: **Nadeen, Nadina, Nadine, Nadja, Nadya, Natka**

Nadira (Arabic) having great value; treasured; a promise

Najla (Arabic) pretty eyes

Treasure

Nancy (Hebrew) elegant; grace *Also*: **Nan, Nanette, Nanna**

Nandana (Hindu) happiness

Nao (Japanese) truthful

Naomi (Hebrew) beautiful; gentle *Also*: **Noemi**

NAOMI

Other "Beautiful" Names for Girls

Adonia (Greek)

Bonnie (Scottish)

Callie (Greek)

Farah (English)

Nani (Hawaiian)

Vashti (Persian)

Wyanet
(Native American)

Beautiful...

Natalia (Latin) birthday of the Lord *Also*: **Natala, Natalie, Nathalia, Nathalie**

Natasha (Greek) born again *Also*: **Natasia, Tashi, Tashia, Tassa**

Nell (English) light *Also*: **Nella, Nelley, Nellie, Nelly**

young girl...

Nicole (Greek) people of victory *Also*: **Nichola, Nichole, Nicki, Nicola, Nicoleen, Nicoletta, Nicolle**

Nina (Spanish) young girl *Also*: **Antonia, Janina**

Noelle (French) joy; Christmas

Nora (Greek) light *Also*: **Noreen, Norina**

Norma (Latin) pattern

Nyssa (Greek) wanting to succeed

Obioma (African) kind

Octavia (Latin) eighth *Also*: **Octavie**

Odele (German) wealthy *Also*: **Odoa, Odeela, Odelia, Odelina, Odell, Odella, Odelyn, Odile**

Odelette (French) little song

N O R M A

Norma Jean Baker was the real first name of actress

a. Lucille Ball

b. Marilyn Monroe

c. Katherine Hepburn

b. Marilyn Monroe

Odelia (Hebrew) praise God *Also*: **Odeleya**

Odette (French) wealthy *Also*: **Odetta**

Odina (Native American) mountain

Odiya (Hebrew) song of God

Okalani (Hawaiian) from the heavens

Oki (Japanese) middle of the ocean

Ola (Polish) protector of people *Also*: **Olesia**

Oleda (English) noble *Also*: **Oleta, Olethea**

Olga (Russian) holy *Also*: **Elga, Olenka, Olia, Olina, Olli, Olunka, Oluska, Olva, Olya**

Olivia (Latin) olive tree *Also*: **Lioa, Liv, Olia, Olive, Olivette, Ollie, Olva**

Olympia (Greek) from Mount Olympus, home of the gods in Greek mythology *Also*: **Pia**

Oma (Arabic) leader

Other "Ocean" Names

Moana (Hawaiian)

Oceana (Greek)

Pelagia (Greek)

Sagara (Hindu)

Thalassa (Greek)

Oksana (Russian) praise to God

Oneida (Native American) looking forward to *Also*: **Onida, Onyda**

Oni (African) something wanted

Onora (Latin) honor

Opal (English) a gem that is rainbowlike in color *Also*: **Opalina**

Ophelia (Greek) helper *Also*: **Ofelia**

Oralie (French) golden *Also*: **Oralee, Oralia, Oriel, Orlena, Orlene**

Orpah (Latin) a fawn *Also*: **Ofra, Ofrit, Ophra, Oprah, Orphy**

Osen (Japanese) thousand

Padma (Hindu) lotus, a kind of water lily *Also*: **Padmini**

Paige (French) someone learning a skill

Paloma (Spanish) dove *Also*: **Palomita, Peloma**

Pamela (Greek) honey *Also*: **Pam, Pamelia, Pamelina, Pammie**

Parvani (Hindu) celebration *Also*: **Parvina**

Patricia (Latin) noble *Also*: **Pat, Patreece, Patria, Patricka, Patrizia, Patsy, Patty, Tricia, Trish, Trisha**

Paula (Latin) small *Also*: **Paola, Paolina, Paulene, Pauletta, Paulette, Paulie, Paulina, Pavla, Pola, Polly**

P I T A

Other "Daughters"

Basia (Hebrew)

Bethia (Hebrew)

Binti (Arabic)

Kaligenia (Greek)

Kanya (Hindu)

Natane (Native American)

Pearl (Latin) small, glossy gem usually rounded and white or bluish-gray in color *Also*: **Pearline, Perl, Perla**

Penelope (Greek) someone who works with bobbins (reels for thread) *Also*: **Lopa, Pela, Pelcia, Pen, Penina, Penna, Peny, Piptisa, Popi**

Phoebe (Greek) brilliant *Also*: **Pheabe, Phebe, Phobe**

Phyllis (Latin) leafy tree branch *Also*: **Philis**

Pita (African) fourth daughter

Polly (English) bitter *Also*: **Pauleigh, Pollee, Pollyanna**

Priscilla (Latin) ancient *Also*: **Pricilla, Pris, Prysilla**

Querida (Spanish) much loved

LOVED

Quinci (English) property belonging to the fifth son
Also: **Quincie**

Quiterie (French) peaceful

R E G I N A

Queens and Princesses

Damita (Spanish) princess

Daria (Persian) queen

Lareina (Spanish) queen

Malka (Hebrew) queen

Zaira (Italian) princess

Rachel (Hebrew) lamb
Also: **Rachael, Rachelle, Rae, Raelene, Raquel**

Radha (Hindu) success

Ragnild (German) power *Also*: **Ragnhild, Ranilda, Renilda**

Ramona (English) wise protector

Rayna (Hebrew) song of the land *Also*: **Raina, Rane, Renana, Renatya**

Queen...

Rebecca (Hebrew) joined together; beautiful *Also*: **Becca, Becky, Reba, Rebecka, Rebekah, Rebi, Rheba**

Regina (Latin) queen *Also*: **Raenah, Raina, Raine, Regine, Reyna**

Renee (French) born again *Also*: **Renata, Rene, Renelle, Reni**

Chapter 3: What's In a Name?

Rhoda (Greek) rose *Also*: **Rhodia, Rhody, Roda**

Rhonda (Welsh) grand *Also*: **Ronda**

Rochelle (French) little rock
Also: **Roshelle**

ROSE....

Rolanda (German) famous land
Also: **Rolande, Rolonda**

Roni (Hebrew) joy
Also: **Ronia, Ronice, Ronit**

Rosalind (Spanish) pretty rose
Also: **Rosalina, Rosalinda, Rosalyn, Roslyn**

Rose (Latin) kind of flower *Also*: **Rosetta, Rosie, Rosita, Ruza**

Rosemary (Latin) dew of the sea *Also*: **Rosemaria, Rosemarie**

Roxanne (Persian) dawn *Also*: **Roxana, Roxie**

R U B Y

Other "Colorful" Names

Garnet (English) red

Melia (Spanish) yellow

Midori (Japanese) green

Iolana (Hawaiian) violet

Saffron (English) yellow

Tale (African) green

Ruby (English) a red gemstone
Also: **Rube**

Ruth (Hebrew) friend *Also*:
Ruthe, Ruthella, Ruthie

friend...

Sabah (Arabic) morning

Sabra (Hebrew) rest

Sabrina (Latin) from the boundary line

Sadzi (Native American) sun heart

Sakae (Japanese) wealth

Salome (Hebrew) peace *Also*: **Saloma, Salomey, Salomi**

Samantha (English) told by God *Also*: **Sam, Samella, Sammee, Sammi, Semantha**

Sandra (English) protector of people *Also*: **Sandee, Sandie, Sandrea, Saundra, Zandra**

Sarah (Hebrew) princess *Also*: **Sadie, Saidee, Salena, Sally, Sara, Sarai, Saretta, Sari, Sarra**

Sasha (Russian) protector of people *Also*: **Sasa, Sascha**

Savannah (Spanish) an area without trees *Also*: **Savanna**

Sawni (Native American) echo

Sayo (Japanese) born at night

Scarlett (English) red

Selena (Greek) goddess of the moon in Greek mythology *Also*: **Celena, Celina, Celine, Salena, Selene, Selinda**

Seraphina (Hebrew) angel
Also: **Sarafina, Serafine**

Serena (Latin) peaceful; calm
Also: **Sarena, Sarina, Serina**

Shahar (Arabic) moonlight

Shaina (Hebrew) beautiful
Also: **Shaine, Shayna**

Shannon (Irish) wise; small *Also*: **Shana, Shannan**

Sharlene (German) woman *Also*: **Sharleyne, Sharlina**

Sharon (Hebrew) a plain *Also*: **Sharan, Sharona, Sharonda, Sharone, Sheron, Sherryn**

Sheba (Hebrew) promised daughter

Sheela (Hindu) gentle

Shelby (English) estate on a ledge *Also*: **Shelbee**

Shelley (English) meadow on a ledge *Also*: **Shellie**

Beautiful...

Shirley (English) bright meadow *Also*: **Shirlene, Shirlynn**

Shizu (Japanese) quiet *Also*: **Shizue, Shizuko**

Shoshana (Hebrew) lily

Sibyl (Greek) prophet *Also*: **Sibella, Sybel, Sybil, Sybyl**

Sierra (English) mountain; saw

Sigourney (French) daring king

Sigrid (Scandinavian) beautiful victory

Siko (African) crying

Simone (French) God listens *Also*: **Simona, Simonette, Symone**

CRYING...

Soledad (Spanish) solitude

Sophia (Greek) wisdom *Also*: **Sofi, Sofia, Sonia, Sophie, Zofia, Zosia**

Stacy (Greek) resurrection *Also*: **Stace, Stacey, Stacia**

Stephanie (Greek) crown *Also*: **Stefania, Steffi, Stevie**

Sukey (English) lily *Also*: **Sukee, Suki**

CROWN...

Susan (Hebrew) lily *Also*: **Susanna, Susanne, Susie, Suzane, Zsa Zsa, Zusa**

Svetlana (Russian) star *Also*: **Svetla, Svetlanka**

Sydney (French) someone from St. Denis, a city in France *Also*: **Sydnee, Sydni, Sydnie**

Sylvia (Latin) from the forest *Also*: **Silvana, Silvia, Silvie, Sylva, Sylvanna**

France...

Tabitha (Aramaic) gazelle *Also*: **Tabby**

Tain (Native American) new moon

Taki (Japanese) waterfall

Talia (Hebrew) dew of heaven
Also: **Talie, Talora, Talya, Thalya**

Tallulah (Native American) leaping
water *Also*: **Talula**

Tam (Vietnamese) heart

Tamika (Japanese) child of the people *Also*: **Tamiko, Tamiya**

Tara (Irish) rocky hill *Also*: **Trah, Taran, Tareena,
Tarin, Teryn**

Tasha (Russian) Christmas *Also*: **Tashina**

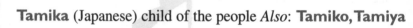

Tate (Scandinavian) bubbly
Also: **Tatum**

Tatiana (Russian) from a
Roman clan name
Also: **Latonya, Tahna,
Tana, Tanis, Tonya**

Tatsu (Japanese) dragon

T A T I A N A

Other Clan Names
Horatia
Portia
Sabina
Sharmaine

Taylor (English) tailor

Teresa (Greek) harvest *Also*: **Teresita, Teri, Terise, Tess, Tessa, Theresa, Thereza, Tracy**

Tessa (Polish) much loved by God *Also*: **Tess, Tessia**

Thaddea (Greek) brave *Also*: **Thada**

Thaleia (Greek) to bloom *Also*: **Thalia**

Thelma (Greek) determination *Also*: **Telma**

Theodora (Greek) gift of God
Also: **Teddy, Teodora, Theda, Theodosia**

Thomasina (English) twin
Also: **Thomasa, Toma, Tommi**

Tiffany (Greek) God's appearance *Also*: **Tiff, Tiffani**

Tish (English) happiness
Also: **Tisha**

Tora
(Scandinavian)
thunder

Trixie (English)
she brings happiness

Ula (Irish) jewel from the ocean

Ulva (German) fox

Uma (English) flax, a blue-flowered plant sometimes used to make cloth

Urit (Hebrew) light

Ursula (Latin) female bear
Also: **Ursella**

Uta (Japanese) song

Valerie (Latin) strong
Also: **Val, Valaria, Valarie**

Vanessa (Greek) butterfly
Also: **Vanesse, Vania, Vanna**

Vanja (Scandinavian) God is good

Veda (Hindu) knowledge

Vera (Latin) truth *Also*: **Veira, Verena, Viera**

Veronica (Latin) truth
Also: **Vernice, Verona, Veronique**

Victoria (Latin) victory *Also*: **Torey, Tori, Toria, Vicki, Vicky, Victorina, Vittoria**

Light and Dark

Adrienne (French) dark

Darcy (Irish) dark

Jelena (Russian) light

Kiara (Irish) dark

Lucinda (Latin) light

Meira (Hebrew) light

Noor (Arabic) light

light

Vida (Hebrew) life
Also: **Veda, Veida, Vidette, Vita**

Violet (Latin) a kind of flower
Also: **Viola, Violetta**

Queen Victoria
ruled over the United Kingdom for 63 years, the longest in British history. She became queen when she was only 18 years old, after her uncle, King William IV, died. The time that she ruled, from 1837 to 1901, is called the Victorian Age.

V I C T O R I A

Virginia (Latin) pure *Also*: **Ginny, Virginie**

Vivian (Latin) full of life *Also*: **Viv, Vivecka, Vivianna, Vivianne, Vivien**

Walda (German) someone who rules *Also*: **Welda**

Wanda (German) someone who wanders *Also*: **Wandi, Wandis, Wonda**

Whitney (English) white island *Also*: **Whitnee**

Wila (Hawaiian) faith

Wilfreda (English) peace *Also*: **Wilfrida**

Wilhelmina (German) constant protector *Also*: **Willa, Wilma**

Willow (English) a kind of tree

Winifred (German) peacemaker *Also*: **Win, Winnie, Wynn**

Winona (Native American) first-born *Also*: **Wenona, Wynonah**

Wynne (Welsh) fair

Xandra (Spanish) protector

Xanthe (Greek) yellow *Also*: **Xantha**

W I L L O W

Other Kinds of Trees

Adoette (Native American) big tree

Alani (Hawaiian) orange tree

Ayla (Hebrew) oak tree

Idra (Hebrew) fig tree

Tamara (Hebrew) palm tree

A kind of tree...

Xaviera (English) new house

Xena (Greek) friendly
Also: **Xenia**

Xin (Chinese) beautiful

Xuan (Vietnamese) spring

beautiful...

Xylia (Greek) forest *Also*: **Xyla, Xylina**

Yachi (Japanese) good luck *Also*: **Yachiko**

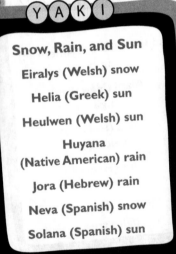

Y A K I

Snow, Rain, and Sun

Eiralys (Welsh) snow

Helia (Greek) sun

Heulwen (Welsh) sun

Huyana
(Native American) rain

Jora (Hebrew) rain

Neva (Spanish) snow

Solana (Spanish) sun

Yaki (Japanese) snow
Also: **Yukie, Yukiko**

Yasmine (Arabic) from the
flower, Jasmine *Also*: **Yasmeen,
Yasmena, Yasmin**

Ye (African) first-born of twins

Yin (Chinese) silver

Ynez (Spanish) pure

Yoki (Native American)
bluebird

Yoko (Japanese) good

Yolanda (Greek) violet flower
Also: **Eolanda, Iolanda, Yalinda, Yola, Yoli**

Yoshiko (Japanese) quiet *Also*: **Yoshi**

Yula (Russian) young *Also*: **Yulenka, Yuliya**

Yuriko (Japanese) lily child

Yvonne (French) young archer
Also: **Yvette**

Zada (Arabic) lucky
Also: **Zaida**

Zalika (African) well born

Zara (Hebrew) dawn *Also*: **Zaria**

Zarina (Hindu) golden

Zehari (Hebrew) bright

Zeldam (German) gray fighting girl

Zhuo (Chinese) smart

Zilla (Hebrew) shadow *Also*: **Zylpha**

Zitkala (Native American) bird

Y U R I K O

Other "Child" Names

Bambi (Italian)

Chavi (English)

Keiki (Hawaiian)

Z I T K A L A

Other Native American "Animal" Names

Chapa — beaver

Doli — bluebird

Inola — black fox

Opa — owl

Sahkyo — mink

Taima — fox

Zoe (Greek) life *Also*: **Zoie**

Zuri (African) beautiful

Zowie (Greek) life

Zuriel (Hebrew) God is my rock

Aanan (Hindu) face

Aaron (Hebrew) raised in power *Also*: **Arek, Aron**

Abdu (Arabic) servant *Also*: **Abduhl, Abdul**

Elvis Presley's middle name was Aaron.

Abraham (Hebrew) father of many *Also*: **Abe, Abram, Abrao, Avraham**

Adam (Hebrew) man of the red earth *Also*: **Adamek, Adamson, Adao**

Adrian (Latin) someone from Adria, a northern city in Italy; dark one *Also*: **Adriane, Adrienne**

Ahmed (Arabic) praise; more deserving *Also*: **Ahmad**

Aidan (Irish) fire; warm

Akihiko (Japanese) bright boy *Also*: **Akio, Akira**

Alan (English) handsome; cheerful *Also*: **Al, Alanson, Alen, Allyn**

Albert (Old German) bright; noble *Also*: **Alberto, Albin, Albrecht**

Alexander (Greek) defender of people *Also*: **Alastair, Alec, Alejandro, Alejo, Aleksander, Alessandro, Alex, Alexandre, Alexandros, Alexei, Allister, Sacha, Sashka**

Alfred (Old English) wise listener
Also: **Alfredo, Avery**

Ali (Arabic) elevated

Andrew (English) brave *Also*: **Andor, Andre, Andreas, Andrei, Andy**

Angel (Greek) messenger of God *Also*: **Angelo**

Anthony (Latin) priceless *Also*: **Andonis, Antin, Antoine, Anton, Antonio, Antony, Antos, Tony**

Other "Bear" Names
Bjorn (Scandinavian)
Dov (Hebrew)
Mahon (Irish)
Orson (Latin)

Arnold (Old German) strong as an eagle *Also*: **Arnie, Arnoldo**

Arthur (Celtic) bear; rock *Also*: **Art, Artair, Arte, Artek, Artie, Arturo**

Ashley (Old English) ash tree meadow *Also*: **Ashton**

Austin (English) majestic *Also*: **Austen, Austyn**

Bailey (English) person in charge *Also*: **Baily, Baylee**

Barry (Gaelic) sharp; something pointed *Also*: **Barrett, Barrymore**

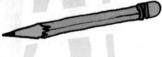

Beau (French) beautiful *Also*: **Beauregard, Bo**

Benjamin (English) son of the right hand *Also*: **Ben, Benjamino, Benji, Benny**

Bernard (German) brave as a bear *Also*: **Barnard, Barnie, Bernardo, Bernhard, Bernie, Burnard**

Blaine (Irish) thin

Blair (Scottish) a flat place *Also*: **Blaire, Blayr, Blayre**

Blake (Old English) pale skin; white *Also*: **Blayke**

Bradley (Old English) a wide meadow *Also*: **Brad, Bradleigh, Bradly**

Brady (Old English) wide island

Brandon (English) sword; on fire *Also*: **Bran, Branden**

Brett (English) someone from Britain *Also*: **Bretton, Britt**

Brian (Celtic) brave; strong *Also*: **Briano, Bryan, Bryant**

B R U C E

Bruce (French) from the brush

Superhero Names

Bruce Wayne
Batman

Clark Kent
Superman

Peter Parker
Spider-Man

Mathew Michael Murdock
Daredevil

Robert Bruce Banner
Hulk

Caleb (Hebrew) brave; dog *Also*: **Kaleb**

Calvin (English) bald *Also*: **Cal, Kalvin**

Cameron (Gaelic) crooked river *Also*: **Camron**

Canute (Scandinavian) knot *Also*: **Knute**

Carl (English) man *Also*: **Karl**

Carlton (English) farmer's land *Also*: **Carleton, Charleton**

Casey (Irish) observant *Also*: **Cayce, Kasey**

Cassidy (Irish) smart *Also*: **Cassady**

Cedric (Welsh) leader of war
Also: **Cedrick, Cedrych**

Chad (English) protector
Also: **Chadwick**

Chandler (English) candle maker

Charles (English) man *Also*: **Carlos, Charlie, Chas, Chip, Chuck**

Christopher (English) one who holds Christ in his heart
Also: **Chris, Christoff, Christos, Cristoforo**

CHANDLER

Maker of...

fire — Bodaway (Native American)

barrels — Cooper (English) and Kiefer (German)

arrows — Fletcher (English)

harnesses — Lorrimer (Latin)

Clark (English) scholar
Also: **Clarke, Clerc**

Clayton (English) house or town near a clay bed *Also*: **Clay**

Clyde (Scottish) from the River Clyde in Scotland

Cody (English) cushion *Also*: **Codie, Coty, Kodey**

Colin (English) victorious people; young boy *Also*: **Cole, Colyn**

Connor (Irish) much desire *Also*: **Conner**

Corey (Irish) the hollow *Also*: **Corin, Korey**

Cornelius (Latin) horn *Also*: **Cornelus**

Cosmo (Greek) order *Also*: **Cosme**

Cullen (Irish) handsome
Also: **Cullin**

Dakota (Native American) friend

Damian (Greek) tame
Also: **Dameon, Damien**

Daniel (Hebrew) God is my judge
Also: **Dan, Daniels, Danilo, Danny**

Dante (Latin) everlasting *Also*: **Dontae, Donte**

HANDSOME...

D A K O T A

Other "Friendly" Names
Alvin (English)
Corwin (English)
Darwin (English)
Delvin (English)
Dovidas (Lithuanian)
Kadin (Arabic)
Lewin (English)

Darin (Greek) gift
Also: **Daron, Darren**

David (Hebrew) cherished *Also*: **Dave, Daveed, Davy**

Dean (English) valley

Deangelo (Italian) from the angel *Also*: **D'Angelo, DiAngelo**

Dennis (Greek) from Dionysus, the god of wine in Greek mythology *Also*: **Denka, Denny, Denys**

Denzil (English) from a town in Britain *Also*: **Karl**

Derek (English) leader *Also*: **Derick, Deryk, Dirk**

Devin (Irish) poet

Dexter (Latin) right-handed

Dimitri (Russian) someone who loves the earth *Also*: **Dimitrios**

Dominick (English) lord *Also*: **Domek, Domenic, Domingo, Nick**

Donald (Scottish) mighty *Also*: **Donaldo, Donny**

Douglas (English) dark water *Also*: **Doug**

Drew (Welsh) wise *Also*: **Karl**

Duane (Irish) dark-skinned *Also*: **Dwayne**

Dustin (German) brave fighter

Dwight (Flemish) white; blond

Other "Blondes"
Boyd (Irish)
Finan (Irish)
Flavian (Latin)
Kenyon (Irish)

Dylan (Welsh) son of the ocean *Also*: **Dillon**

Dark Skinned..

Earl (English) leader *Also*: **Errol**

Edward (English) wealthy protector *Also*: **Ed, Eddie, Eduardo**

Elmo (German) protector

Elvis (Scandinavian) all wise

Emmett (German) powerful *Also*: **Emmot**

Enrico (Italian) leader of the house *Also*: **Enrique**

Eric (Scandinavian) ruler of the people *Also*: **Erick, Erik**

Ethan (Hebrew) strong *Also*: **Etan**

Etienne (French) a crown

Eugene (Greek) well born
Also: **Eugenio, Gene**

ETIENNE

Crowns and Helmets

Anakale (Hawaiian) crown

Caffar (Irish) helmet

Coryell (English) helmet

Stamos (Greek) crown

Taj (Hindu) crown

Evan (Welsh) God is good;
young warrior
Also: **Evans, Ewan**

Fabian (Latin) someone
who grows beans
Also: **Fabek, Faber,
Fabiano, Fabio, Fabius**

Fareed (Hindu) unique

Felipe (Spanish) lover of horses

Felix (Latin) happy; lucky

Fergus (Irish) best choice
Also: **Ferris**

Ferguson (Irish) son of Fergus

Finian (Irish) fair

Floyd (Welsh) gray hair

Forbes (Scottish) field

Forrest (French) woods *Also*: **Forester, Foster**

Francis (French) someone from France *Also*: **Francisco,
Franco, Francois, Frank**

Franklin (English) property owner *Also*: **Frank, Frankie, Franklyn**

Franz (German) someone from France *Also*: **Frans, Franzl**

Fraser (English) curly hair *Also*: **Fraze, Frazer**

Frederick (German) leader of peace *Also*: **Fred, Freddie, Frederico, Friederich, Fritz**

Gabriel (Hebrew) God is my strength *Also*: **Gabe, Gabo, Gavi**

Galen (Greek) peaceful

F R A S E R

Other "Hairy" Names

Brendan (Irish) smelly hair

Caesar (Latin) long hair

Ciaran (Irish) black hair

Clancy (Irish) red hair

Crispin (Latin) curly hair

Esau (Hebrew) hairy

Ferrand (French) gray hair

Reed (English) red hair

curly hair...

G A R E T H

King Arthur's Knights

Gawain

Lancelot

Percival

Tristan

Gareth (Welsh) gentle; a knight from the legends of King Arthur

Garrett (English) brave with a spear

Garth (Scandinavian) gardener

Gary (English) spear

Gavin (Welsh) white falcon *Also*: **Gavan, Gawaine**

Gene (English) well born

George (Greek) farmer *Also*: **Georges, Giorgio, Jorge**

G I D E O N

Other "Warrior" Names

Balin (Hindu)

Calhoun (Celtic)

Gunther (Scandinavian)

Mordecai (Hebrew)

Gerald (German) ruler with a spear *Also*: **Geraldo, Gerry, Jerald, Jerry**

Gideon (Hebrew) great warrior *Also*: **Gidon**

Gilbert (German) bright pledge *Also*: **Gilberto**

Giles (Greek) young goat; shield *Also*: **Gil, Gyles**

Glenn (Irish) narrow valley

Gordon (English) round hill *Also*: **Gordy**

Gore (English) spear

Grady (Irish) famous

Graham (English) gray home *Also*: **Gram**

Grant (Latin) great

Gregory (Latin) observant *Also*: **Greg, Gregor, Greig**

Griffin (Latin) someone with a hooked nose *Also*: **Griff, Griffon**

Guy (French) leader; guide *Also*: **Guion**

Hai (Vietnamese) sea

G O R D O N

Gordon Matthew Sumner is the real name of singer

a. **Moby**

b. **Mick Jagger**

c. **Sting**

c. Sting

58

Hakeem (Arabic) wise *Also*: **Hakim**

Halbert (English) bright hero

Hari (Hindu) tawny

Harold (English) army ruler
Also: **Hal, Haroldo**

Harrison (English) son of Harry

Harry (English) ruler at home

Harvey (French) eager for battle

Hashim (Arabic) destroyer
of evil *Also*: **Hasheem**

Hayden (English) hill of heather;
hedged place *Also*: **Aidan, Haden, Haydn**

Hector (Greek) holds fast *Also*: **Hektor**

Henry (German) ruler of the house *Also*: **Henri, Henrik**

Herbert (German) shining army *Also*: **Herb, Herbie**

Other Heroes
Conlan (Irish)
Sweeney (Irish)
Dooley (Irish)

wise...

HENRY

Henry was a very popular name for kings. England had eight, France and Germany both had three.

Hershel (Hebrew) deer
Also: **Herschel**

Howard (English)
observer

Hugh (English) wise *Also*: **Huey, Hughes**

Hunter (English) huntsman

Ian (Scottish) God is good
Also: **Ean, Ianos**

Ichabod (Hebrew) lost glory

Ignatius (Latin) on fire
Also: **Iggy, Ignacio**

Ilario (Italian) cheerful

Ira (Hebrew) observant;
descendant

Innis (Scottish) island

Irving (English) sea friend
Also: **Irv**

Isaac (Hebrew) laughter *Also*: **Isaak**

Isaiah (Hebrew) God helps me *Also*: **Isa**

Ishmael (Hebrew) God will hear *Also*: **Ismae**

Israel (Hebrew) struggle with God

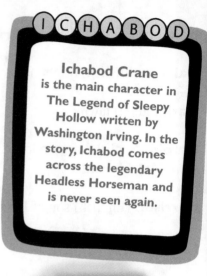

ICHABOD

Ichabod Crane is the main character in The Legend of Sleepy Hollow written by Washington Irving. In the story, Ichabod comes across the legendary Headless Horseman and is never seen again.

JACOB

In the United States, Jacob was the most popular name for baby boys born in the years 1999–2002.

Ivan (Hebrew) God's gift
Also: **Ivanek, Ivano**

Jacob (Hebrew) supplanter;
held by the heel *Also*: **Jaco,
Jake, Jakub**

Jafar (Arabic) river *Also*: **Gafar**

Jamal (Arabic) handsome *Also*: **Gamal, Jamahl, Jameel**

James (English) he who replaces; supplanter; held by the heel *Also*: **Jacques, Jaime, Jim, Jimmy**

Jameson (English) son of James *Also*: **Jamison**

Jared (Hebrew) descend *Also*: **Jarad, Jerrod, Yared**

Jason (Hebrew) God is my salvation *Also*: **Jace, Jayson**

Jay (Latin) blue jay; jaybird *Also*: **Jae, Jaye**

Jeffrey (German) peace *Also*: **Geoff, Geoffrey, Jeff**

Jeremy (Hebrew) the Lord exalts *Also*: **Jemmie, Jeremias, Jerimiah, Jerry**

Jermaine (German) someone from Germany *Also*: **Jermain**

Jerome (Greek) sacred name

Jesse (Hebrew) wealthy *Also*: **Jessie**

J A M E S

Jameses, Jims, and Jimmys

James Bond — secret agent

James Dean — actor

Jimmy Buffet — singer

Jim Carey — actor

Jimmy Fallon — comedian

Jim Morrison — singer

Jimmy Neutron — cartoon character

WEALTHY...

J A C K

Jack is #1!
Jack, a form of the name John, is a very popular name.

England 1994 to 2002

Wales 1999 to 2002

Ireland 2000 and 2001

Scotland 2002

Jesus (Hebrew) the Lord is my salvation

Ji (Chinese) order

Joel (Hebrew) God is Lord; Jehovah is God

John (Hebrew) God is good *Also*: **Jack, Johann, Johnnie, Jovan, Juan**

61

Jonathan (Hebrew) gift from God/Jehovah *Also*: **Jon, Jonny**

Jordan (Hebrew) to descend *Also*: **Jorden, Jordy**

Joseph (Hebrew) God will increase *Also*: **Jody, Jose, Josef**

Joshua (Hebrew) God is my salvation *Also*: **Josh**

Julius (Latin) young *Also*: **Julian, Julio**

Justin (Latin) fair *Also*: **Justino, Justo**

Kacey (English) he announces peace

Kadir (Arabic) capable

Kahil (Turkish) young *Also*: **Cahil, Kaleel**

Kane (Welsh) beautiful *Also*: **Kain, Kayne, Keanu**

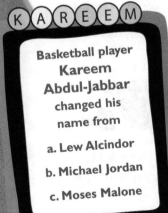

K A R E E M

Basketball player
**Kareem
Abdul-Jabbar**
changed his
name from

a. Lew Alcindor

b. Michael Jordan

c. Moses Malone

a. Lew Alcindor

Kareem (Arabic) generous
Also: **Karim, Karime**

Karl (German) man *Also*: **Karlen**

Kay (Welsh) joy

Keaton (English) hawk nest; place
name *Also*: **Keeton, Keyton**

FOREST...

Keith (Scottish) forest

Kelby (German) a farm by a spring *Also*: **Kelby**

Kelly (Irish) warrior *Also*: **Kellie**

Kelsey (English) island; place name

Kendrick (English) royal hero
Also: **Kendricks, Kendrik**

Keneke (Hawaiian) handsome
Also: **Keneti**

Kenji (Japanese) second son

Kenneth (Irish) handsome
Also: **Ken, Kendall, Kenny**

Kevin (Irish) handsome; small;
gentle *Also*: **Kev, Keven**

Kirk (Scandinavian) church
Also: **Kirke**

Other Islands
Carlisle (English)
Ellery (English)
Holmes (English)
Rodney (English)

Handsome...

Kurt (German) bold; wise

Kyle (Scottish) narrow land
Also: **Ky**

Lamar (Latin) the sea
Also: **Lemar**

Lambert (German)
bright land

Lane (English) narrow path
Also: **Laine, Layne**

Kurts in Sports
Kurt Ainsworth Baseball
Kurt Browning
Figure skating
Kurt Busch Driver
Kurt Schulz Football
Kurt Warner Football
Kurt Wastell
Snowboarding

Langston (English) long town

Lawrence (Latin) crowned with laurel *Also*: **Larry,
Laurence, Laurencio, Loren, Lorenzo**

L E V I

In 1873, **Levi Strauss** from Bavaria and Jacob Davis, a tailor from Nevada, came up with the world's first pair of jeans. These popular jeans are still sold all around the world!

Lee (English) meadow *Also*: **Leigh**

Leif (Scandinavian) beloved *Also*: **Lief**

Leon (Greek) lion *Also*: **Leo**

Leonard (German) bold as a lion *Also*: **Lennard, Lenny, Leonardo, Lonnie**

Levi (Hebrew) attached; joined to *Also*: **Levon**

Liam (Irish) determined protector

Logan (Irish) from the hollow

Louis (French) famous warrior *Also*: **Lotario, Lou, Luigi, Luis**

Lucas (Latin) bringer of light *Also*: **Lukas, Luke**

Ludwig (German) well-known soldier

Madison (English) son of the mighty warrior *Also*: **Maddie**

Mahmoud (Hindu) worthy *Also*: **Mahmood, Mahmud, Mehmoud**

Malcolm (English) a servant

L U D W I G

Imagine having to compose music you can't hear! **Ludwig Van Beethoven** did just that. Beethoven began composing when he was about 10, but he started losing his hearing when he was in his twenties. His hearing loss did not stop him from creating some of the most popular classical music we still listen to today.

Marcellus (Latin) young warrior *Also*: **Marceau, Marcel, Marcello**

Marcus (Latin) warlike *Also*: **Marco**

Mark (Latin) warlike
Also: **Marc, Marco, Markos**

Marshall (French) someone
who cares for horses
Also: **Marschall**

WARLIKE

Martin (Latin) warlike *Also*: **Mart, Martel, Martie, Martino, Marto**

MICHAEL

Michaels in Sports

Michael Andretti — racecar driver

Mike Bibby — basketball

Mike Bossy — hockey

Michael Jordan — basketball

Mickey Mantle — baseball

Mike Modano — hockey

Mike Piazza — baseball

Marvin (English) famous friend; friend of the sea *Also*: **Marv, Marvyn**

Matthew (Hebrew) gift of God *Also*: **Mateo, Mathew, Matias, Matt**

Maurice (Latin) dark-skinned *Also*: **Mauricio, Maury, Morice, Morry**

Maxime (Latin) great

Michael (Hebrew) who is like God *Also*: **Micah, Michele, Mick, Mickey, Miguel, Mikael, Mike, Mikhos, Mitch, Mitchell**

Montgomery (English) rich man's mountain

Moses (Hebrew) saved from the water

Muhammad (Arabic) greatly praised *Also*: **Ahmad, Amed, Hammad, Mehemet, Mohammed, Muhamoud**

Murray (Scottish) mariner

Nabeel (Arabic) noble *Also*: **Nabil**

Nadim (Hindu) friend *Also*: **Nadeem**

Nadir (Arabic) having great value; a promise

Najib (Arabic) smart *Also*: **Najeeb**

Nathan (Hebrew) gift from God *Also*: **Nat, Natan, Nate, Nathaniel, Nathen**

M U H A M M A D

Boxer **Muhammad Ali's** name before he changed it was

a. Jack Johnson

b. Cassius Marcellus Clay

c. Rocky Marciano

b. Cassius Marcellus Clay

FRIENDS...

N A T H A N

In 1916, **Nathan Handwerker** opened a hot dog stand on Coney Island, New York, where he sold hot dogs for a nickel. Today, every July fourth people come from around the world to Coney Island to compete in Nathan's Famous hot dog eating contest.

Navarro (Spanish) land *Also*: **Navarre**

Neil (Irish) champion *Also*: **Neal, Nigel, Niles, Nilo**

Nelson (English) son of Neil *Also*: **Neilson**

Nestor (Greek) traveler

Nicholas (Greek) people of victory; victorious people *Also*: **Niccolo, Nick, Nicolai, Nicolas, Nikky, Nikolos, Nikos**

Noah (Hebrew) rest

Noel (French) joy; Christmas

NOEL

Because of its meaning, many people with the name Noel share the same birthday—December 25!

Nocona (Native American) wanderer *Also*: **Nokoni**

Norman (English) someone from the north *Also*: **Norm, Normando**

Nuru (African) light

Obadiah (Hebrew) servant of God *Also*: **Obadias, Obe, Obie**

ORVILLE

Orville Redenbacher started popping corn on his family's farm when he was just a kid. He was so interested in popcorn that he spent years experimenting with it until he got the light, fluffy popcorn we munch on today.

Octavius (Latin) eighth child *Also*: **Octavian, Octavio**

Oliver (Latin) olive tree *Also*: **Olivero, Olivier, Ollie**

Omar (Arabic) follower of the prophet

Orlando (Spanish) famous land

Orville (French) town of gold

FAMOUS LAND......

Osborn (English) divine bear

Oscar (Scandinavian) divine spear *Also*: **Oskar, Ossie**

Owen (Welsh) well born *Also*: **Owain**

Pablo (Spanish) little

Palmer (English) carrying palm branches; one who holds a palm

PALM...

Paine (Latin) a man from the country

Palmer (English) someone who holds a palm leaf or branch

Parker (English) park keeper *Also*: **Parke**

Patrick (Latin) noble man *Also*: **Paddy, Pat, Patric**

Paul (Latin) small *Also*: **Pablo, Paolo, Pasha, Paulo, Puly**

Percy (French) peace of the valley

P E T E R

Well-Known Peter's
Peter Forsberg hockey
Peter Pan book character
Pierre-Auguste Renoir artist
Pete Rose baseball
Pete Sampras tennis
Peter Warrick football

Peter (Greek) rock *Also*: **Pearce, Pearson, Pedro, Petey, Petras, Petro, Pierce, Pierre, Pierson, Pietro, Pyotr**

Philip (Greek) someone who loves horses *Also*: **Felipe, Phil, Phillipe**

Preston (English) a priest's town

Price (Welsh) son of an ardent man; son of Rhys *Also*: **Pryce**

Pryor (Latin) church leader

Quentin (Latin) fifth child *Also*: **Quent, Quint, Quinten, Quito**

Quincy (French) estate of the fifth son; fifth

Quinn (Irish) wise

Radcliff (English) red cliff

Rahim (Hindu) compassionate

Ralph (English) wolf-counselor *Also*: **Ralphie, Raul, Rolph**

Randolph (English) wolf with a shield *Also*: **Randall, Randey, Randolf**

Raphael (Hebrew) God has healed *Also*: **Raffaello**

Rashid (Arabic) righteous *Also*: **Rasheed**

Raymond (English) protector *Also*: **Raimundo, Ramon, Ray, Raymund, Reimond**

Reece (Welsh) zealous *Also*: **Reese, Rhys**

Reginald (English) strong counselor *Also*: **Reggie**

Remy (French) from Rheims, a town in central France *Also*: **Remi**

Rene (French) born again *Also*: **Renato, Rennie**

Reuben (Hebrew) Behold, a son *Also*: **Ruben**

Reynold (English) powerful advisor *Also*: **Renaldo, Renault, Reynolds**

Richard (German) strong ruler *Also*: **Dic, Ricardo, Rich, Rick, Rico, Ritchie**

Riley (Irish) brave *Also*: **Reilly**

(R)(O)(R)(Y)

Other "Colorful" Names

Aswad (Arabic) black
Dwight (Flemish) white
Harkin (Irish) dark red
Lavan (Hebrew) white
Odhran (Irish) pale green
Oran (Irish) green
Porfirio (Greek) purple
Taman (Slavic) black

Robert (English) bright fame *Also*: **Bob, Bobby, Rob, Robby, Roberto, Roberts, Robin, Rubert**

Roger (German) well-known spearman *Also*: **Rodger, Rogelio, Rutger**

Roland (German) famous land *Also*: **Rrolle, Rollins, Rowland**

Ronald (English) powerful advisor; decisive ruler *Also*: **Ron, Ronnie**

Rory (Irish) red

Ross (English) woods; red

Roy (French) king

Ryan (Irish) little king

Saed (Arabic) lucky; happy *Also*: **Saeed, Said, Saiyid, Sayid**

Salvatore (Latin) savior *Also*: **Sal, Salvador**

Happy...

70

Other "Lucky" Names

Asad (Arabic)

Balabhadra (Hindu)

Faust (Latin)

Fortino (Latin)

Masud (Arabic)

Prospero (Latin)

Wapi (Native American)

Samuel (Hebrew) God has heard *Also*: **Sam, Sammy, Samuello**

Sanjay (Hindu) winner

Saul (Hebrew) asked for

Scott (English) someone from Scotland *Also*: **Scotty**

Sean (Irish) God is good *Also*: **Shaine, Shane, Shaun, Shawn, Shayne**

Sebastian (Latin) from Sebastia, a city in ancient Rome

Seth (Hebrew) to appoint

Seymour (French) from St. Maur, a village in France *Also*: **Seamour**

Shahzad (Hindu) son of the king

Shannon (Irish) old; wise

Sharif (Hindu) respected *Also*: **Shareef**

Shelby (English) place near the edge

Sheldon (English) steep valley *Also*: **Shelden**

Sheridan (Irish) wild man *Also*: **Sheridon, Sherridan**

Simon (Hebrew) God hears *Also*: **Simeon, Simms, Simone, Symon**

Skip (Scandinavian) boss of a ship *Also*: **Skipp, Skipper, Skippy**

Solomon (Hebrew) man of peace *Also*: **Salom, Selim, Shlomo, Sol, Solly**

Spencer (English) someone responsible for supplying food and drink *Also*: **Spence**

Stanley (English) stony meadow *Also*: **Stan, Stanlee**

Stephen (Greek) crowned *Also*: **Stefan, Stefano, Stephanos, Stepka, Stevan, Steve, Steven, Stevenson, Stevie**

Stewart (English) someone responsible for supplying food and drink
Also: **Stu, Stuart**

Sullivan (Irish) having black-colored eyes *Also*: **Sullavan**

Sylvester (Latin) forested
Also: **Silvestre, Sly**

S T E V E

Steve Hillenberg is the creator of the cartoon SpongeBob SquarePants. Other creators and their cartoons are:

Walt Disney • Mickey Mouse

Matt Groening • The Simpsons

William Hanna • Scooby Doo

Chuck Jones • Bugs Bunny

Tad (Welsh) father *Also*: **Tadd**

Tam (Vietnamese) eight

FOREST...

Tanner (English) someone who works with leather
Also: **Tan, Tanier**

Tate (English) happy *Also*: **Tait, Tayte**

Taylor (English) tailor

Terrence (Latin) smooth
Also: **Terencio, Terrance, Terry**

Thaddeus (Aramaic) brave
Also: **Taddeo, Thad**

Theodore (Greek) gift from God *Also*: **Ted, Teddy, Teodoro, Theo, Theodor**

THEODORE

Theodore was the first name of author Dr. Seuss. His full name was Theodore Seuss Geisel.

Thomas (Arabic) twin
Also: **Tam, Thom, Thomson, Tom, Tomas, Tomasso, Tuomo**

Timothy (Greek) honoring God
Also: **Tim, Timmy, Timon**

Tobias (Hebrew) God is good
Also: **Tobe, Tobey, Tobiah, Tobin**

Todd (English) fox

Torrance (Irish) little hills
Also: **Torin, Torrence, Torrey**

Toshiro (Japanese) skillful

Travis (French) someone who collects tolls *Also*: **Travers, Travys**

Trevor (Welsh) large homestead *Also*: **Trefor, Trev, Trevis**

Turner (English) someone who works with wood

Tyler (English) someone who makes tiles *Also*: **Ty**

Tyrone (Irish) land of Owen *Also*: **Tirone**

Tyson (English) firebrand

Ulmer (English) famous wolf *Also*: **Ulmar**

Ulysses (Latin) extremely angry *Also*: **Odysseus**

Uberto (Italian) very smart *Also*: **Hubert**

In Greek mythology, Ulysses was king of Ithaca. He fought in the Trojan War, which lasted for 10 years. When the war was finally over, it took him another 10 years to return home. The many adventures he had during his return trip are told in the poem *Odyssey*, written by the Greek poet Homer.

SMART...

Uri (Hebrew) light *Also*: **Uriel**

Valerian (Latin) healthy; strong *Also*: **Val, Valerio**

Vance (English) marshland *Also*: **Van, Vancelo**

Vanya (Russian) God is good *Also*: **Vanek, Vanka**

Vaughn (Welsh) small

Venturo (Spanish) good luck

Victor (Latin) conqueror *Also*: **Vic, Victorino, Victorio, Viktor, Vittorio**

Vincent (Latin) the winner *Also*: **Vikent, Vin, Vince, Vincente, Vincenzo, Vinci, Vinnie**

Vito (Latin) alive

Vladimir (Russian) famous ruler *Also*: **Vlad, Vladimeer, Vladlen**

THE WINNER...

Volker (German) protector of the people

Wade (English) to cross the river

Wagner (German) wagon maker

Waldo (German) strong; someone who rules

Wallace (English) someone from Wales *Also*: **Wallach, Wallie, Wallis, Wally, Welsh**

WARWICK

What's Near What?

Bemidii (Native American) river by a lake

Brigham (English) village near a bridge

Clifton (English) town near a cliff

Digby (English) farm by a ditch

Marlow (English) hill near a lake

Rodney (English) island near a clearing

Walcott (English) cottage by the wall

Walter (German) ruler of the people *Also*: **Walt, Walther, Watkin**

Warren (German) protector; observer *Also*: **Warrin, Warriner**

Warwick (English) house near a dam *Also*: **Warrick**

Wayne (English) wagon maker *Also*: **Wain, Wainwright**

Wendell (German) wanderer *Also*: **Wendel, Wedle**

Wesley (English) western meadow *Also*: **Wes, Wesly, Westley**

Wilbur (German) brilliant *Also*: **Wilber, Wilbert**

Other "Guardians"

Eamon (Irish)

Edek (Polish)

Hafiz (Arabic)

Kenward (English)

Norward (English)

William (German) constant protector *Also*: **Bill, Billy, Guillaume, Guillermo, Vas, Vaska, Vilhelm, Will, Willem, Willie, Willis, Wilson, Wilhelm**

Winston (English) friend's town *Also*: **Winton, Wynston**

Wolfgang (German) wolf fight

Woodrow (English) row by the woods *Also*: **Woody**

Wyatt (French) small fighter *Also*: **Wiatt**

Wycliff (English) white cliff

Xanthus (Greek) blond *Also*: **Xanthos**

Xavier (English) new house *Also*: **Saverio, Xaver**

Xenos (Greek) friendly; guest

Friendly...

Wolfgang was the first name of one of the world's best-known composers of music — Wolfgang Amadeus Mozart.

WOLFGANG

Xerxes (Persian) king

Yadid (Hebrew) much loved

Yair (Hebrew) God will teach
Also: **Jair**

Yamal (Hindu) one of a twin

Ye (Chinese) universe

Yen (Vietnamese) calm

Yo (Chinese) bright

York (English) yew
tree *Also*: **Yorrick**

X E R X E S

Kings, Princes, and Lords

Abhiraja (Hindu) king

Creon (Greek) prince

Ithel (Welsh) lord

Regan (Irish) king

Rex (Latin) king

Tiernan (Irish) lord

TWIN...

Y A M A L

Other "Twins"

Akwetee (African)

Chumo (Spanish)

Tavish (Irish)

Tomlin (English)

Yosef (Hebrew) God increases
Also: **Yusif, Yuzef**

Youri (Greek) farmer

Yukiko (Japanese) snow *Also*: **Yuki, Yukio**

Yves (French) yew wood *Also*: **Yvon**

Zachariah (Hebrew) remember God *Also*: **Zach, Zacharias, Zacharie, Zachary, Zeke**

Zaki (Arabic) pure

Zale (Greek) strong like the sea

Zane (English) God is good *Also*: **Zayne**

Zareb (African) guardian

Zesiro (African) first-born of twins

Zhu (Chinese) wish

Zion (Hebrew) guarded land; highest point

Zuriel (Hebrew) God is my rock

Chapter 4

What About Your Last Name?

Thousands of years ago, when there weren't hundreds of Emilys or Alexanders, people were known by just one name. Then the world became more crowded. It was harder to know which Henry you were talking about when there were three boys with that name living in the same village. So, sometime in the 11th century, people started using last names, or surnames.

Thanks to surnames, there was no more confusing Olive Hammond with Olive Lacey. Surnames were passed down from generation to generation. Now people could tell what family you were from by knowing your last name.

So it's not only your first name that means something. Your last name can mean something, too. It can tell you where in the world your ancestors came from, and it might also tell you what they did for a living. For example, the last name "Guerin" comes from an Old French word that means to "watch" or "guard". So if that's your last name, maybe your ancestor was a guard in a French castle!

On the next few pages you'll read more about the five main ways people used to create the family names we have today. (Some surnames are so well liked that they've become popular first names. If you don't find your last name in this chapter, try looking in Chapter 3.)

1. Sons (and Daughters) of the Father

Surnames based on the father's name were easy to make, and they are very common. These names were made by adding a suffix to the end of the father's name, or by adding a prefix to the beginning of the father's name. People in different countries used different suffixes and prefixes. In most places, both girls and boys used the same surname even though it means "son of." (Think "child of" instead.)

In England, they added "son" or "kin" to the father's name.
Harry + son = Harrison (son of Harry)
William + kin = Wilkin (little William)

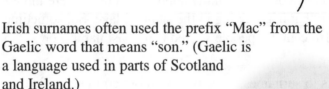

In Scandinavia, "sen" was used.
Hans + sen = Hansen (son of Hans)

Irish surnames often used the prefix "Mac" from the Gaelic word that means "son." (Gaelic is a language used in parts of Scotland and Ireland.)
Mac + Donald = Macdonald

Sometimes Irish names added the prefix "O" which means grandson. "O" was added to a grandfather's name.
O + Connell = O Connell (grandson of Connell)

The Welsh added "ap" before the father's name to create a surname. Evan, who is the son of Harry, is *Evan ap Harry*. On occasion the "ap" was combined with the father's name. For example, *ap Harry* is now the surname Parry, and *ap Howell* (son of Howell) is now Powell.

SURNAME	COUNTRY	WHOSE SON?
Alvarez	Spanish	Alvaro
Davis	English	David
DeLuca	Italian	Luca
Evans	English	Evan
Fernandez	Spanish	Fernando
Gonzales	Spanish	Gonzalo
Harris	English	Harry
Henderson	English	Henry
Hughs	English	Hugh
Murphy	Irish	descendant of a sea warrior
Lopez	Spanish	Lope
McIntyre	Scottish	son of the carpenter
Nelson	Irish	Nell (or Neil)
Olson	Scandinavian	Olef
Ortiz	Spanish	Orta
Ramirez	Spanish	Ramiro
Valdez	Spanish	Baldo

2. What Did He Look Like?

If your last name is Russell, it could be because your father's, father's, father's, father's, father's, father had red hair. (Russell mean "red hair" in French.) This kind of surname could give you clues about what your ancestors looked like!

SURNAME	COUNTRY	FEATURES
Braun	German	brown skin, hair, or clothes
Campbell	Gaelic	crooked mouth
Kennedy	Gaelicugly	ugly
Klein	German	short
Krause	German	curly hair
Lang	English	very tall
Moreno	Spanish	dark skin or hair
Reed	English	red face or hair
Ricci	Italian	curly hair
Schwarzkopf	German	black hair

A person's personality, or a particular characteristic, might also be the source of a surname.

SURNAME	COUNTRY	CHARACTERISTIC
Lustig	German	happy
Fuchs	German	clever (from fox)
Gallo	Italian	proud (from rooster)
Stammler	German	stutterer

3. I Live Near a Cottage

You have two friends named Julie. One of them lives near the park, and the other lives in a gray house. If your talking with your parents about the first Julie, you might say, "You know Julie, the one who lives near the park."

Surnames based on where someone lived started something like that. Everyone kept saying, "Hey, there's Julie Marino," which is really like saying, "Hey, there's Julie who lives by the ocean." Pretty soon, everyone knew her as Julie Marino.

SURNAME	COUNTRY	LIVED NEAR OR CAME FROM
Burnes	English	river or a stream
Aguilera	Spanish	from the city of Aguilas, Spain
Castillo	Spanish	castle
Cruz	Spanish	cross
DuBois	French	the woods
Fleming	Norman	from Flanders, an area in Western Europe
Hall	English	large manor house
Hayes	English	fenced off area used for hunting
Ives	English	from St. Ives, a town in England
Lombardi	Italian	from Lombardy, an area in Italy
Marino	Italian	the sea

... chart continued on page 84

SURNAME	COUNTRY	LIVED NEAR OR CAME FROM
Mendoza	Spanish	from Mendoza (cold or high mountains)
Moore	English	moor
Munro	Gaelic	from Ro
Murray	Scottish	from Moray, an area in Scotland
Peña	Spanish	large rock
Rios	Spanish	river
Romano	Italian	from Rome, Italy
Scott	Scottish	from Scotland
Soto	Spanish	from Soto (various places with that name in Spain)
Sutherland	Scottish	from the south land
Torres	Spanish	tower

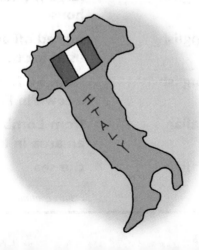

4. Guess What My Job Is

Want to know what your ancestors did way back then? Maybe your last name lets you know. Many surnames were created from a person's job.

SURNAME	COUNTRY	WHAT THE PERSON DID
Baker	Saxon	bake
Carter	English	carry goods by cart or wagon
Columbo	Italian	care for doves
Foster	French	make scissors
Garner	French	take care of a silo (a place where people store corn)
Hoffmann	German	farm land he owns
Marshall	French	work with horses
Miller	English	work in a grain mill
Myers	English	doctor
Parker	English	take care of wild animals
Schmidt	German	blacksmith
Schneider	German	tailor (someone who makes clothes)
Smith	English	blacksmith
Wagner	German	made wagons
Werner	German	watchman
Zimmerman	German	carpenter

5. Lots of Different Reasons

Sometimes, last names were picked because the person liked the way the word sounded, or he liked what the word meant in his language.

SURNAME	COUNTRY	MEANING
Chavez	Portuguese	keys
Diaz	Spanish	days
Doherty	Scottish	obstructive
Esposito	Italian	to put outside; often given to children who were abandoned
Forbes	Gaelic	field
Irving	Scottish	green water
Jung	German	young
Kaiser	German	king
Lambert	English	bright land
Lee	Chinese	plum tree
Mancini	Italian	left-handed
Neumann	German	new settler; newcomer

young

Chapter 5

Your Pirate Name, Wild West Name, and More

Now that you know what your name means, how about coming up with a pirate name? On the next few pages, you can answer a few questions, or use the letters in your name to come up with a pirate name and more!

What's Your Pirate Name?

If you love digging for treasure and greet everyone with an "Ahoy!" then all you need is a pirate name. Take the quiz and then follow the instructions to find out what your fellow pirates should call you.

Real Pirates

Blackbeard

Henry Morgan

Anne Bonny

Mary Read

"Calico Jack" Rackham

William Kidd

1. Parrots and monkeys are the best kinds of pets to have.
   A. Of course! (go to question 2)
   B. I'll stick with dogs, cats, or fish. (go to question 5)

2. Your friends would describe you as stubborn and always ready to argue.
   A. So what if I like to argue? (go to question 3)
   B. I get along with everyone. (go to question 5)

3. You get seasick riding in a car going over a bridge.
   A. Water is not my friend. (go to question 5)
   B. I never get seasick! (go to question 4)

4. You wouldn't mind if all of your friends were always a little... stinky.
   A. The smellier, the better! (go to question 7)
   B. Ugh! I don't like bad smells. (go to question 5)

5. You would love to spend the summer at the beach.
   A. I love the sand and water. (go to question 6)
   B. No thanks. My skin burns easily. (go to question 6)

6. You make a great leader.
A. My friends trust I always know what I'm doing.
(go to question 7)
B. Everyone knows I get lost trying to find my bedroom.
(go to question 7)

7. You prefer the color
A. red. (go to **Your Pirate Name**)
B. black. (go to **Your Pirate Name**)

Your Pirate Name

Now pick one (just one!) of the questions.
What answer did you choose for that question?
Look at the chart below to see what your pirate name is.

QUESTION	YOUR ANSWER	YOUR PIRATE NAME
I	A	Buccaneer (your last name)
	B	(your first name) the Ordinary
2	A	(your first name) the Quarrelsome
	B	Mild (your first name)
3	A	Green-Faced (your last name)
	B	(your first name) the Fierce
4	A	(your first name) the Smelly
	B	(your first name) the Looter
5	A	Caribbean (your first name)
	B	Landlubber (your first name)
6	A	Captain (your first name)
	B	Hopeless (your first name)
7	A	(your first name) Redhook
	B	(your first name) Black

What's Your Wild West Name?

Wish you could be a cowhand, riding your horse and helping to bring in the cattle? Until you learn to rope and get yourself a horse, you can start with a name that at least makes you sound like you belong in the Wild West.

To get your Wild West name, find the row in the first chart that has the first letter in your first name. Look under **Cowgirls** if you're a girl, or under **Cowboys** if you're a boy. This is your western first name.

Then find the row in the second chart that has the third letter of your last name. This is your western last name. Put both names together for your full Wild West name. (*Example: If your name is Steve Murphy, your Wild West name is Gage West.*)

FIRST LETTER OF YOUR FIRST NAME	COWGIRLS	COWBOYS
A, B, C	Cheyenne	Billy
D, E, F	Hallie	Dillon
G, H, I	Sheridon	Cody
J, K, L	Dayle	Jesse
M, N, O	Annie	Eli
P, Q, R	Luz	Wyatt
S, T, U	Peyton	Gage
V, W, X	Hallie	Hunter
Y, Z	May	Austin

THIRD LETTER OF YOUR LAST NAME	
A	Starr
B	Lee
C	Laramie
D	Blaze
E	Sloan
F	Carson
G	Hughston
H	Lane
I	Larado
J	Dallas
K	Avery
L	Fields
M	Oakley
N	Earp
O	Rider
P	Earl
Q	Landon
R	West
S	Harper
T	Sierra
U	Denver
V	Sage
W	Zane
X	Yates
Y	Derringer
Z	Stetson

cowgirl!....

What's Your Secret Agent Name?

Can you stay cool under pressure? Do you always have to have the latest, greatest gadget? Can you break a code? Is your dream to be a secret agent?

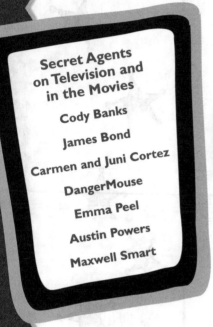

Secret Agents on Television and in the Movies

Cody Banks

James Bond

Carmen and Juni Cortez

DangerMouse

Emma Peel

Austin Powers

Maxwell Smart

secret AGEnt...

Read each statement below. If the statement describes you, check true. If the statement doesn't describe you, check false. Then look under **Your Secret Agent Name** to see what your code-name is.

1. You're excellent at keeping secrets.
_____ true _____ false

2. You and your friends are always talking in code so no one else can understand what you're talking about.
_____ true _____ false

3. You're never without your dark glasses.
_____ true _____ false

4. You would love to travel to different places. The farther, the better!

_____ true   _____ false

5. You have a great memory. If you see it or hear it once, you don't forget.

_____ true   _____ false

6. You speak with a British accent. (Or you can fake it if you try.)

_____ true   _____ false

7. You are great with computers and electronic gadgets.

_____ true   _____ false

8. You have had martial arts training since you were little.

_____ true   _____ false

9. You love to dress in disguise so no one can recognize you.

_____ true   _____ false

10. You are clever—you can quickly come up with a solution to a problem.

_____ true   _____ false

Your Secret Agent Name

Answered mostly true? You're almost ready for the covert world of espionage. Of course, first you'll need to complete years of training. But, until you're finished, keep your secret agent name handy:

Agent (initial of your first name)-(your age)

(*Example*: *If your name is Ryan and you're 9 years old, your secret agent name is Agent R-9.*)

Answered mostly false? Maybe you're not quite ready to be a secret agent. But, if you insist, try something simple like "Junior Agent Bob" or "Junior Agent Tina".

What's Your Wizard Name?

You would probably love it if you could finish your homework, take out the trash, or set the table with just a wave of a wand. Unfortunately, life isn't that simple. But if you can't be a wizard, saying *abracadabra* to clean up your room, you can at least go around feeling magical with a wizardly name.

To get your wizard name, find the row in the first chart that has the first letter in your first name. The word in the column next to that letter is the first part of your new name.

Then find the row in the second chart that has the second letter of your last name. The word in the column next to that letter is the second part of your name. Put both parts together for your full wizard name.
(*Example*: *If your name is Miranda Johnson, your wizard name is Filiamusca.*)

FIRST LETTER OF YOUR FIRST NAME	
A, B, C	Val
D, E, F	Mor
G, H, I	Sol
J, K, L	Tibi
M, N, O	Filia
P, Q, R	Vir
S, T, U	Letum
V, W, X	Noctu
Y, Z	Avis

SECOND LETTER OF YOUR LAST NAME	
A, B, C	nix
D, E, F	lumen
G, H, I	semper
J, K, L	sidus
M, N, O	musca
P, Q, R	natio
S, T, U	pulcher
V, W, X	dred
Y, Z	magus

This Book Belongs To

_____

My Name Means

_____

_____

_____

_____

_____

_____

_____

_____

_____